You Are Very Special

You are very Special

Su Box

Illustrations by Susie Poole

LION
Children's Books

Text by Su Box
Illustrations copyright © 1996 Susie Poole
This edition copyright © 2000 Lion Publishing

Published by
Lion Publishing plc
Mayfield House, 256 Banbury Road,
Oxford OX2 7DH, England
www.lion-publishing.co.uk
ISBN 0 7459 4269 5

First hardback edition 1996
First paperback edition 2000
10 9 8 7 6 5

A catalogue record for this book is available
from the British Library

Printed and bound in Singapore

This book is about someone very special.
It is all about y<u>ou</u>.

Here is a space for your name:

Amy Fairfield

Think of someone you love.
Mum, Dad, or a special friend.
Did you know–you are special, too?

The world is full of people–
big and small, black and white.
But God made you just as you are,
and he made you just right.

God made all of you,
from the top of your head
down to your toes.
He made all of you—your eyes,
your ears, your mouth and nose.

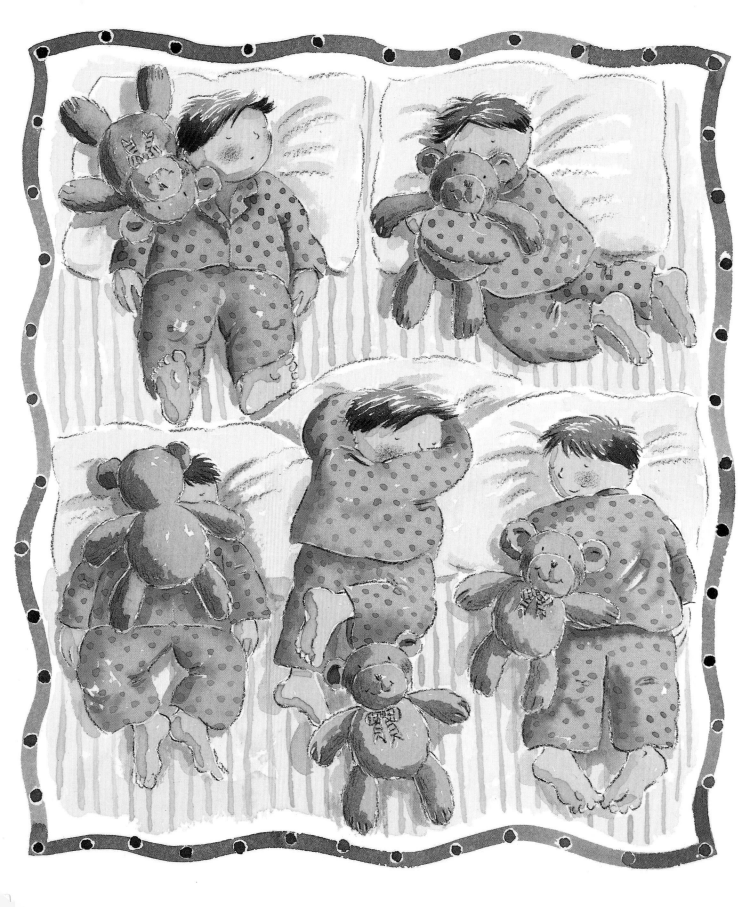

Can you hear yourself breathing?
Can you feel your heart beating?
Did you know your body works
even when you're sleeping?

Look at the pattern on your fingertip.
Nobody else has a pattern like yours.
You're not the same as <u>anyone</u> else.
Don't you think that's special?

Some children like to run and shout.
Other children sit and dream.
Some children are always busy.
Which one is most like you?

Being special doesn't make you good!
Sometimes you do things that make
people sad.
But when you say "Sorry", you can
be friends again.

Everyone is special to someone.
People show they care in different ways—
by giving a hug or by what they say.
How are you made to feel special?

You are special to all your friends,
and God wants to be your friend, too.
He already knows you very well,
and he cares about you.

God wants us to care for each other.

He made the world that way.

How do you show someone you love them?

How do you make them feel special?

So many things make you special.
Can you think what a really special person
might look like?
Close your eyes for a moment and imagine...

Now turn the page...
and what can you see?

Here is a very special person.
This special person is y<u>ou</u>!

**Other books for young children
from Lion Publishing**

Bartimouse Aboard the Ark Christina Goodings

Henry's Song Kathryn Cave

In the Beginning Steve Turner

Sleepy Jesus Pennie Kidd

When the World Was New Alicia Garcia de Lynam